STOP
OVERthinking

chartwell
books

STOP
OVERthinking

A Workbook to STOP PERFECTIONISM,
PEOPLE PLEASING, SELF-SABOTAGE, and
Other Forms of **NEGATIVE THINKING**

TINA TESSINA, PH.D., L.M.F.T.

chartwell
books

CONTENTS

YOU *CAN* CHANGE YOUR THINKING HABITS

You picked up this book because you're concerned about overthinking. Maybe you find that ruminating about something that's upset you interferes with your productivity or ratchets up your anxiety levels. Or perhaps you've experienced one of the biggest problems of overthinking: difficulty getting to sleep or staying asleep. Overthinking is dysfunctional, like a mental stutter or tremor, hampering your ability to get around mentally, or think clearly. The good news is that you aren't stuck with it. This book is a prescription for healing overthinking and converting your thought process to an effective and productive use of your excellent brain.

What is Overthinking?

Overthinking is nonproductive; it usually goes round and round in circles that lead nowhere, generates or adds to your stress or tension, and is generally a waste of mental energy—in other words, an emotional drain. Overthinking solves nothing and gets in the way of your solving problems or enjoying things. Overthinking feels like it's driving you crazy, and it won't leave you alone. It hampers productivity, adds stress to whatever is going on, and wastes a lot of time you could be using in more productive and enjoyable ways.

You'll know you're overthinking when you feel overwhelmed, or your mind feels that it's on a loop. Maybe you have work problems you can't leave at work, so you mentally bring them home and never shut them off. However, the endless ruminating you do about work does nothing to help solve the problems, and it builds tension and prevents sound sleep. Or you get stuck in overthinking about how to do something, to the point that you can't do it at all. Perfectionism (a type of overthinking) can cause you to want things to be so perfect, you can never finish them. If you have children (which is an awesome responsibility), you can get so overwhelmed by overthinking, you either overprotect your children, or you feel paralyzed and incapable of parenting them.

Women are significantly more likely than men to fall into overthinking and to be immobilized by it. In fact, according to a study from the University of Michigan, 57 percent of women and 43 percent of men classify themselves as overthinkers. But no matter who is troubled by overthinking, they will benefit from the corrective process in this workbook.

The Good News

The good news is that overthinking can be conquered and converted into productive and enjoyable mental processes. *Stop Overthinking* is designed to help you overcome every type of overthinking and convert it into healthy and calm thinking that will actually reduce your stress, improve your sleep patterns, and help you accomplish your goals. As you read it, you'll find prompts and exercises that will help you tackle each type of overthinking in a productive way and convert your toxic habits into fruitful, healthy thinking. You'll also find helpful information, such as statistics and research, and supportive and illuminating quotations and affirmations in each section to guide you along the way.

> Overthinking has reached epidemic proportions: nearly three-quarters of those 25 to 35 years old overthink, as do about half of those age 45 to 55.

This workbook can also help you:

▶ **Reduce stress:** You'll learn how to observe your mental process without obsessing and worrying fruitlessly.

▶ **Reduce worry and anxiety:** You'll learn how to face your fears and conquer them, meaning, you won't have to worry about them anymore.

▶ **Focus your attention:** You'll learn how to focus on one thing at a time, which helps you to keep track, figure out what you want to know, and achieve your goals.

▶ **Organize your thoughts:** Once you've focused, you can then get your thoughts into a logical order.

▶ **Order your thinking:** When your thoughts are focused and organized, you can write things down and prioritize them into a step-by-step plan.

▶ **Improve your well-being:** Calming your racing thoughts reduces stress, expresses pent-up emotions, and helps you think clearly about them so you can decide what you want to do.

▶ **Make time for yourself:** Writing the answers to these prompts is like a love letter to yourself, and it makes it clear that you care about you, which is a boost to healthy self-esteem.

Stop Overthinking is organized in the same way I work with clients with these problems. Most of the prompts are based on questions I ask my clients and the "homework" I give them, which is designed to teach mental management skills. Each section is based on one type of overthinking, which are outlined in the coming pages.

The steps are progressive, so it's best to begin with the first one and continue through to the end—including the exercises that don't seem to address the kind of overthinking that troubles you. As you continue your journey, you'll start to notice a difference very quickly because you'll find prompts designed to help you manage your thoughts and your mind in a new way, which will have a noticeable effect in a short time. You'll find that you're more comfortable with your inner thoughts and feelings, calmer, less tense, and happier. Your sleep will also improve.

Make this the workbook for creating the life you want. Explore yourself and improve your mental outlook through these self-reflective writing prompts. There's no way to make a mistake here, and the only one who'll see your written musings will be yourself. Let's begin.

> According to a study in the *European Journal of Social Psychology*, habit formation can take as little as 18 days—and as many as 254 days. The researchers found the average amount of time needed for a behavior to become automatic is 66 days.

"The greatest weapon against stress is our ability to choose one thought over another."

—William James, father of modern psychology

1. HOW OVERTHINKING AFFECTS YOUR HEALTH, YOUR HAPPINESS, AND YOUR LIFE

There are several direct ways overthinking can affect your health, which is why it's so important to get a handle on it. As noted, overthinking can interfere with sleep, but it can also create stress and lead to or deepen depression.

Overthinking and Sleep Deprivation

▶ If you have ever lain awake at night, feeling like you can't shut your mind up, overthinking has affected your sleep. Overthinking can prevent you from sleeping or even resting, which, of course, your brain needs to operate at its best. If this goes on for long enough, you can suffer from sleep deprivation.

Your brain/mind wants to be active 24/7, even when you're sleeping. Your brain uses sleep to process the day's information and sort through it. If you don't give your brain some guidance and enough rest, it can make up ways to be active; overthinking is one of the toxic ways it will do so, if you don't guide it.

Consider sleep deprivation experiments, where people who were kept awake for days had psychotic breaks because their brains developed hallucinations and paranoia. In 1959, radio DJ Peter Tripp (among others) challenged himself to stay awake on air. YouTube videos show that after staying awake for 200 hours, he started seeing fire where there was none and thought his PR people were dangerous to him.

While this might seem like a PR stunt with short-term effect, sleep deprivation from overthinking has serious health consequences; the longer it goes on, the more serious the consequences become. Science has linked poor slumber with a number of health problems, from weight gain to a weakened immune system. When you sleep well, your body heals itself and restores its chemical balance. Your brain forges new thought connections and helps memory retention. If overthinking disturbs your sleep, your brain and body systems won't function normally. It can also dramatically lower your quality of life.

Sleep deprivation can affect your mind and body with:

- ▶ Memory issues
- ▶ Mood changes
- ▶ Trouble with thinking and concentration
- ▶ Being accident prone (including car and industrial accidents)
- ▶ Weakened immune system
- ▶ High blood pressure
- ▶ Risk for diabetes
- ▶ Weight gain
- ▶ Low sex drive
- ▶ Risk of heart disease
- ▶ Poor balance

Other psychological risks of sleep deprivation include:

- ▶ Impulsive behavior
- ▶ Anxiety

- ▶ Depression
- ▶ Paranoia
- ▶ Suicidal thoughts

If sleep deprivation from overthinking is severe enough, you could start having hallucinations: seeing or hearing things that aren't really there. A lack of sleep can also trigger mania in people who have bipolar mood disorder. Many of these effects also make the overthinking worse, so it becomes a downward spiral.

Overthinking and Stress

Constant mental churning of negative or fearful thoughts creates stress. Life has sufficient stress that we can't control and must deal with; this self-induced stress has no other cause than overthinking. The physical effects of stress are quite similar to those of sleeplessness, but stress happens mostly while we're awake.

According to the Cleveland Clinic, "When a person has long-term (chronic) stress, continued activation of the stress response causes wear and tear on the body." This wear and tear can lead to the development of physical and emotional symptoms, as well as unhealthy behavioral symptoms that are sometimes used to manage chronic stress.

Physical symptoms of stress include:

- ▶ Headaches and other aches and pains
- ▶ High blood pressure
- ▶ Chest pain or a feeling like your heart is racing
- ▶ Muscle tension or jaw clenching
- ▶ Trouble sleeping, low energy, or exhaustion
- ▶ Dizziness or shaking
- ▶ Digestive issues
- ▶ Sexual problems (e.g., low libido)
- ▶ Weakened immune system, leaving you vulnerable to viruses and infections

Emotional and mental symptoms of stress:

- ▶ Irritability
- ▶ Anxiety or panic attacks
- ▶ Feeling overwhelmed or hopeless
- ▶ Depression

Behavioral symptoms of stress:

- ▶ Drinking alcohol (too much or too often)
- ▶ Smoking
- ▶ Using drugs
- ▶ Overeating or developing an eating disorder
- ▶ Compulsively participating in sex, gambling, or shopping

Your mind/brain and body are equipped to deal with normal, life-induced stress. In fact, a modest amount of stress is helpful, it's energizing, and it activates the immune system. The normal stresses of life are usually short-term, but the stress induced by overthinking is chronic and long lasting. It's a shame that the self-inflicted stress caused by overthinking can produce these results.

Overthinking and Depression

Normal stress response is meant to handle the effects of stress for the short term, but long-lasting chronic stress taxes our physiological stress response beyond what it's designed to do, and it starts to have negative effects on the mind and body.

The effects of chronic, or long-term, stress can be harmful on their own, but they also can contribute to depression, a mood disorder that makes you feel sad and disinterested in things you usually enjoy. Depression can affect your appetite, your sleep habits, and your ability to concentrate.

THE STRESS-DEPRESSION CONNECTION

Stress affects depression, and depression increases stress. It's a destructive cycle, with each increasing the effects of the other.

Research shows that stress has direct effects on mood. The initial symptoms can include irritability, sleep disruption, and cognitive changes, such as impaired concentration. However, the indirect effects of stress are often what causes depression to take hold.

People under stress often stop exercising, connecting with friends and loved ones, and getting enough sleep and relaxation, which depresses mood—and makes depression worse. **For example:** Stress at work can lead to overworking; as a result, the person doesn't go to yoga class, go running, read before bed, or catch up with close friends as much—which can make the person feel more stressed or depressed.

The surprising thing—and the good news for us—is that overthinking is not difficult to fix.

Healthy Thinking as Opposed to Overthinking

Let's begin by contrasting overthinking and healthy thinking. Reminiscing, thinking things through, and problem-solving are all healthy ways to use your brain. As you read through this, see if you can recognize some thought patterns of your own.

REMINISCING

Reminiscing is thinking about past events, feelings, and scenarios. It's often pleasant and nostalgic, but it may involve rethinking some past actions or events so that you don't repeat them or are able to handle them better next time. While pleasant reminiscing is usually delightful, it can sometimes be sad if loved ones are gone or the good times have passed. It tends to leave you with feelings of gratitude for having had the experience and, perhaps, nostalgia for past times that won't happen again. But it generally feels good. If it involves rethinking past events that you wouldn't want to repeat, or things you didn't say, or wanted to say or do better, that's productive problem-solving; as you figure out solutions, it should leave you with a feeling of satisfaction.

THINKING THINGS THROUGH

Thinking things through is something we do when we're not sure we understand what happened or when something is coming up in the future that we feel somewhat unprepared for, and we want to come up with a method of doing, confronting, or presenting. Thinking things through should be relatively calm and detached, using the problem-solving part of the brain to understand and manage something that hasn't happened yet or something that recently happened and was confusing. Some examples include planning a trip or event, preparing a presentation, conceiving of this book, or anticipating an encounter that didn't go well last time and figuring out what to do differently. It's different from obsessive overthinking or ruminating (other types of overthinking) because it is purposeful and usually leads to a resolution.

PROBLEM SOLVING

Problem solving is more intense thinking, tightly focused on some issue that needs to be corrected, done better next time, or figured out in some way. It takes mental energy and can be tiring, but it feels productive and purposeful—and it has a goal. Examples of problem solving might be planning a schedule or project at work, figuring out how to approach a thorny issue from a different perspective, solving a relationship problem as a couple, or working together with a team to tackle a problem. It is intense and can be frustrating at times, but it is goal focused and usually feels productive.

AFFIRMATIONS, PRAYER, REPETITION, AND MEMORIZATION

There are other healthy, repetitive uses of the mind. Affirmations are positive thoughts you repeat to yourself to change your mindset from negative to positive. Prayer is acting on faith, requesting help or giving thanks for life issues. Repetition is a way to fix a thought in your mind, to memorize it. Memorization is great exercise for the brain, creating definitive pathways in long-term memory. All these forms of thinking are useful, productive, valuable, and mentally healthy. They are all good exercises for the mind and brain, and there is some evidence that these types of thinking can help avoid dementia, other brain problems connected with aging, or other types of disordered thinking. Often, stuttering and other disturbed speech patterns can improve by learning more ordered thinking.

Types and Origins of Overthinking

Going forward, this book is divided into ten sections, each one tackling a different type of overthinking or its origins. Most of us will have some experience with all types/origins of overthinking but only be really troubled by a few. However, clearing up all the types will really free your mind for productive and satisfying thought processes. Here are the main types of overthinking.

WORRY/ANXIETY

Worry is having disorganized, fearful thoughts about what could happen, with no focus on solving the problems. Like most forms of overthinking, worry is a series of random thoughts that run through your mind ceaselessly, making you anxious and tense, without fixing the issue. Anxiety is chronic worrying, which loses focus on whatever thing you were worried about and becomes generalized. Unaddressed, anxiety can lead to anxiety attacks, those frightening episodes that seem to come out of nowhere, make your heart pound, and cause you to panic.

PERSEVERATION

Perseveration is having the same thoughts (usually negative) over and over and not being able to let go of them.

PERFECTIONISM

Perfectionism is a specific kind of worry: being anxious that you must be perfect and that you won't live up to your own standards of perfection. This type of thinking is often the result of growing up around a perfectionist.

OBSESSIVE THINKING

Obsessive thinking is like perseveration but more intense. You think the same thoughts over and over, and your mind can't focus on anything else. Obsessive thinking can be paralyzing, stopping you from functioning mentally. The obsessive thoughts can create obsessive behaviors like counting or uncontrollable handwashing.

AVOIDANCE

Avoidance is thinking a lot of random thoughts to avoid feeling or thinking about something unpleasant. It is a major component of Post-Traumatic Stress (PTS) because the feelings associated with trauma can be overwhelming. The main problem with avoidance is that it sets up a fight between your psyche, which wants to express and explore the traumatic event and its associated feelings, and the urge to avoid focusing on those things, which leaves your mind in turmoil.

PEOPLE PLEASING

People pleasing is a less-recognized kind of obsessive thinking, focused on what other people think about you or want from you. When you are constantly worried about what others say or imagining what they are thinking or what will please them, you will have trouble knowing your own opinion.

SELF-SABOTAGE

Self-sabotage is having constant negative thoughts about yourself and what you're doing, and constantly predicting a negative outcome of whatever you're trying to accomplish. Self-sabotage can lead to an unwillingness to do anything, because it's no use, it won't work, or you're not worth it. None of these thoughts are true, but they may sound true.

**In addition to tackling each type of overthinking,
we'll delve into a few underlying causes.**

RESOLVING THE ORIGINS OF OVERTHINKING

Overthinking is the product of your history. Some of it may be learned: if you grew up with a worrier or a perfectionist, you may have learned to think the way they do. It can also arise from trauma, when something terrible happens, and you are fearful that it will happen again, or you're blaming yourself for it. Understanding where the habit comes from will help you overcome it.

REPLACING TOXIC THINKING

Learned behavior is insidious if it's negative. Because you learned it in the past, you may not even realize that it is counterproductive or that there is another way to behave or think. What we experience as children, or when we're vulnerable, can overwhelm us and create toxic thinking without our being aware of it. Rooting out the sources of this learned behavior to replace toxic thinking is a way to overcome it.

OVERTHINKING YOUR OVERTHINKING

Oddly enough, it's possible to turn your overthinking on itself and ruminate, perseverate, or worry about your overthinking, in which case, it becomes a spiral, dragging you down and creating stress—but not doing anything to overcome the problem.

Take Your Time with the Prompts

As you work your way through this book, take your time with each type of overthinking and each prompt. I never ask my clients to do them all at once. It's a learning process, so do it one step at a time, and go back and repeat prompts if it seems helpful. While some of the types of overthinking might not seem to trouble you, I do recommend you try the first two prompts for every type to make sure you're changing all of your overthinking patterns. If the first two prompts of any type of overthinking don't produce results, you can skip that one and go on to the next. The good thing is that you'll have this book to return to if that type rears its ugly head in the future.

"Our fatigue is often caused not by work, but by worry, frustration and resentment."

—Dale Carnegie, *Stop Worrying and Start Living*

2. STOP WORRY AND ANXIETY

Worry is having disorganized, fearful thoughts about what could happen, with no focus on solving the problems. These thoughts can be focused on real things like "I'm worried about the presentation or project I have to do for work," or more fantastic things like "What if I develop a fatal disease?" or "What if the roof falls in?"

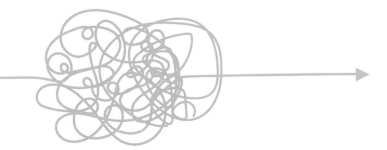

▶ Worry, like most forms of overthinking, is a series of random thoughts (in this case, scary ones) that run through your mind ceaselessly and make you anxious and tense. Even if you're worried about something real, the worry does nothing to fix the issue.

Anxiety is chronic worrying, which loses focus on whatever thing you were worried about and becomes generalized. The free-floating nature of anxious thinking is sneaky because it's hard to pin down and reality check it. Unaddressed, anxiety can lead to anxiety attacks. In this chapter, we'll address both worry and anxiety.

Part I: Stop Worry

When you can't sleep or when you experience anxiety attacks, working through this step can be especially effective. If you worry a lot, or obsessively think about future events and problems when you should be concentrating on other things, follow these prompts. Sit with them for a few minutes and take your time answering.

What do you worry about most often?

_____

_____

_____

_____

_____

_____

_____

_____

_____

_____

_____

_____

_____

_____

_____

_____

How often do you worry or feel anxious?

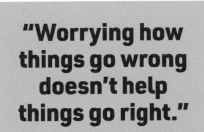

"Worrying how things go wrong doesn't help things go right."

−Karen Salmansohn, author

What does your worry or anxiety feel like?

_____

_____

_____

_____

_____

_____

_____

_____

_____

_____

_____

_____

_____

_____

_____

Everyone experiences stress and anxiety at some point. What's the difference? Stress is a response to a specific danger in a situation, whereas anxiety is a reaction to stress.

_____

_____

_____

_____

_____

_____

If you're feeling anxious or worried, or you can't stop thinking about some event that hasn't happened yet, take a few moments to write down whatever is worrying you. If you can't write it down, think it through carefully until you can clearly say what you're worrying about. Clarifying your worries will stop the free-floating sensation of anxiety with no basis.

Make a list here of your most troublesome worries.

EVALUATE THE WORRY

Think about the first item on your list of worries. Ask yourself, "Is there anything I can do about it now?" If you're at home and worrying about the office, or if the problem won't occur until next week or next year, you may not be able to do anything about it right now. Or you may be worrying about a problem you can do something about, such as calling someone, or getting a cost estimate, or making a doctor's appointment to check out a worrisome symptom.

Write what you can do about your worry.

FOLLOW THROUGH

If there is something you can do, do it. Sometimes, worry is a way to procrastinate, but often, worry is a way to keep a mental list going, as in, "I'm worried that I'll forget to bring the slides for the presentation tomorrow." Consider these examples:

- ▶ If you're worrying about how your presentation will go at work tomorrow, go over your notes and lay out your clothes for the morning.

- ▶ If you're worried about a health problem, look up the illness or injury on a reputable website (like the Mayo Clinic), or contact your doctor and ask some questions. (Note: Be careful that the advice you get from the Internet is from a credible site; don't just believe everything you read.)

- ▶ If you're at work worrying about cooking dinner when you get home, write down a menu or a list of ingredients you need to pick up.

- ▶ If you're worried that you may be fired, update your résumé and call some recruiting or job-search agencies. You don't have to take another job, but if there's a real problem, you'll be prepared.

- ▶ If you're worried that the roof may leak the next time it rains, start making a list about what you can do about it.

Let's take this last one and explore it further to see how this process can work. Your inner dialogue might sound like this:

"The news said it was going to rain next week. I'm worried that the roof might leak."

"Call a roofing company and have them look at it."

"I'm worried that a roofing company will charge me more than they should because I don't know how much it should cost."

"Call my brother (or my neighbor, or my friend) who had his roof done, and ask him what it costs, and also if he liked the contractor he used."

"Okay."

When you reach this "okay" moment, it's time to make the call, or, if it's too late at night, make a note to call the next day—but make sure you follow through and actually make that call.

**Think about that first item on your worry list.
Write your action plan here.**

_____

_____

_____

_____

_____

_____

_____

_____

_____

_____

_____

_____

_____

_____

_____

_____

_____

_____

_____

_____

_____

DISTRACT YOURSELF

When you've done what you can, or made your lists or notes, then distract yourself. Get busy doing something else: clean a room, read, or take a walk or a bath. It will jog your mind out of its habitual track and refresh your thinking, if you allow it. Breaking your train of thought gives you a chance to change it.

_____

_____

_____

_____

_____

_____

_____

DEVELOP A GOOD HABIT

Repeat the previous steps every time you catch yourself worrying. Repetition will help make this process second nature whenever a worry creeps up.

Recap the steps you used here and remind yourself how you know when you're worrying.

_____

_____

_____

_____

_____

_____

Notes

> **"Anxiety does not empty tomorrow of its sorrows, but only empties today of its strength."**
>
> —Alexander McLaren, minister

Part II: Stop Anxiety

Anxiety is what happens when worry is not dealt with and becomes chronic. If you can't sleep, you worry a lot, you "ruminate" or obsess about negative possibilities, startle easily, or you're frequently irritable or needy, you are probably anxious.

WHAT TO DO IF YOU'RE HAVING AN ANXIETY ATTACK

If you have an elevated heart rate, shallow and rapid breathing, and racing thoughts, you're having an anxiety attack. This is a physical response to being scared, but in this case, if you're not actually being threatened with harm, what you're scared of are your own thoughts. Try counting to ten, slowly. This will shift you from your emotional brain (amygdala) to your thinking brain (pre-frontal cortex), which should calm down your body's reactions. You can also breathe into a small paper bag; as you're inhaling carbon dioxide, your heart rate will slow. Or you can talk to yourself calmly and remind yourself there is no present danger, it's only worry or memories that are triggering you. Throughout this book are Quick Calm tips that can help you calm down quickly.

Write down what calming techniques work best for you here.

_____

_____

_____

_____

_____

_____

_____

_____

_____

BECOME AWARE OF YOUR ANXIOUS STATE

What are the feelings, thoughts, and habits (like nail biting, scratching, sighing a lot, or fidgeting) that tell you that you're anxious? Have you noticed that other people call attention to something you might not realize you do, like twirling your hair or rapidly tapping your foot under the table? I have a tendency to loudly sigh a lot when I'm worried, and my husband sometimes calls it to my attention. Unconscious eating, where you devour food that isn't really what you want, is another sign of anxiety.

Write your telltale habits or feelings here.

WRITE DOWN WHAT YOU'RE ANXIOUS ABOUT

Whether your anxiety is based on something happening now (like a troubling health symptom), something that happened in the past (like a relationship breakup or trauma), or something you fear will happen in the future (like financial trouble), give yourself a chance to understand and express your fear. Allow yourself some time to complain and be unhappy about the situation.

Writing down your fears "traps" them on paper (or the computer screen or the phone) and gives you a chance to see them clearly. Once you see them, some of them will stop scaring you, simply because you can see they're not real. The others are now set down where you can evaluate them and figure out what you want to do.

Think of as many negative feelings and thoughts as you can. A health symptom can make you fearful that you'll meet the fate of someone else who had a big health problem; for example, my dad died of a heart attack at 58, and as I approached that age, I was consumed with worry. A past breakup or trauma can cause you to worry that your current relationships will have problems; for me, my early divorce created worries that I'd never love again. And financial woes can make you afraid about your future; like a lot of people, when I felt financially insecure, I would replay a "bag lady" image and terrify myself.

Express as many of the negative feelings and thoughts as possible here. (You may need more paper or a few tries to get it all out.)

EVALUATE YOUR FEARS AND COMPLAINTS

Allow yourself some time to consider the points you made in your list on the previous page. Is there anything you can do differently (and do you want to)? In the case of my divorce fears, I took some relationship workshops and went into therapy to learn better information about how to have a good relationship, and I've now been happily remarried for 40 years. Are you thinking clearly about the problem? Have you considered all the choices you can? If you have a choice, do you still want to change things? If you don't have a choice, can you see some different ways of looking at the problem? Are you resisting unnecessarily? Do your options look different to you now? You might even consider whether you are angry at anyone specifically. To process my fears related to my dad's death when I was 18, I had to get angry at him, and at God, before I could resolve my grief. I got stuck at not wanting to be angry, and it took me ten years to finally face my anger and grief.

Write about your fears and complaints here.

_____

_____

_____

_____

_____

_____

_____

_____

_____

_____

_____

_____

_____

BEFRIEND YOURSELF TO BUILD TRUST

Discuss the problem with yourself as helpfully as you would with a friend. Brainstorm for ideas, realistic or silly, about what you could do to make things better. For example:

- ▶ I could move to Timbuktu and avoid the whole thing.
- ▶ I could talk to Harry and see if he can help me think this through.
- ▶ I could ask Martha to help.
- ▶ I could find a genie and have him make this all better.
- ▶ I could win millions in the lottery and be able to buy my safety.
- ▶ I could go on with my life, doing the best I can, and trust that God will take care of me.

Write your ideas here.

_____

_____

_____

_____

_____

_____

_____

_____

_____

_____

_____

_____

_____

_____

_____

CHECK THE FACTS

Anxiety is often based on confusion, misunderstanding, being negative, or not having good information. In the case of my dad's death, I thought I was supposed to suppress grief, especially the anger part. It was a great relief to finally express it. Do whatever you can to check the facts of the situation and consider all the possibilities for taking care of yourself and those you love. Since my dad essentially worried himself to death, I learned how not to worry (hence, this book).

Write your facts here.

_____

_____

_____

_____

_____

_____

_____

_____

_____

_____

_____

_____

_____

_____

_____

QUICK CALM

Concentrating on almost anything other than your stress can work wonders for your mood. Close your eyes and slowly count to 10—or 20—or count backward once you reach whatever number you're counting to. You can also try saying the alphabet backward.

REVIEW AND DECIDE

Once you've 1) expressed your anger and disappointment, 2) evaluated your feelings, 3) brainstormed ideas, and 4) checked the facts, you will be feeling much more in charge of yourself and this situation. For example, with my financial fears, I had to realize that being on my own at 18 was terrifying. Then

1. I had to express those fears.

2. I had to reality check my fears, and I realized that I had already survived them. I wasn't rich, but I was living comfortably.

3. I figured out what I needed to do to improve my financial condition. I stopped working as a waitress and got an office job with benefits.

4. I learned to budget and move up in my new job.

Review what you've discovered and write your new decisions here.

_____

_____

_____

_____

_____

_____

_____

_____

_____

_____

_____

_____

_____

SELL YOURSELF ON A POSITIVE OUTCOME

Think of all the possible great outcomes of the changes you're making by following those four steps. Consider what you will discover from learning how to confront your worries and plan for success. For me, I realized that if I got myself a better job with benefits, I could relax a lot about money, I could build a career and advance in it, and I could have a bright future.

Figure out how you can maximize the benefits of making the change. When you've convinced yourself, make a commitment to your plan and write your promise to yourself here.

_____

_____

_____

_____

_____

_____

_____

_____

_____

_____

_____

_____

_____

_____

_____

_____

_____

POST AND FOLLOW YOUR PLAN

Draw up a plan for making the best possible results come out of these new mental habits. Put the plan where you can see it and read it every day. Do your best to follow the plan so you'll feel safe. After I got my first good office job, I kept pushing to advance until I was actually told by someone in human resources, "We don't promote women beyond this point." It was 1966, and I found another job. If your plan is clear, obstacles won't stop you.

RECAP AND REPEAT

Just as with the worrying prompts, repeat these steps whenever you feel anxious, until you develop a habit of calming yourself and facing your anxiety. We'll come back to these steps again:

1. Express your anger and disappointment.

2. Evaluate your feelings.

3. Brainstorm ideas.

4. Check the facts.

Recap your own short version of the steps here, to help you remember.

_____

_____

_____

_____

_____

_____

_____

_____

_____

_____

Notes

"Change the changeable, accept the unchangeable, and remove yourself from the unacceptable."

–Denis Waitley, *Seeds of Greatness*

3. STOP PERSEVERATION

Perseverance, a word similar to a word you might be more familiar with, means sticking to something until you succeed. In psychology, the term *perseveration* means having the same thoughts (usually negative) over and over and not being able to let go of them. It is also called ruminating. This often happens when something has upset you and you're helpless to change it.

▶ We often perseverate when someone betrays us or hurts our feelings, or when something that's important to us doesn't go our way. We run the scenario over and over in our minds, looking for a way to change something or someone, but in vain. These prompts will help you to convert perseveration into productive thinking.

Identify the Thought

What scenarios do you replay in your mind frequently? These could be very old events, where you're still trying to get the right outcome or answer from someone, or more current events that you haven't be able to figure out. In my case, I replayed the problems in my first marriage over and over.

Write a list of those scenarios here.

_____

_____

_____

_____

_____

_____

_____

_____

_____

_____

_____

_____

QUICK CALM

Any physical activity helps release stress. Take a 10-minute timeout and do some jumping jacks, take a walk around the block, ride your bike, or rake the yard.

_____

_____

_____

_____

_____

_____

_____

_____

_____

_____

If you find that you ruminate, try getting out into a natural environment like a beach, walking trail, or park (as opposed to something manmade, like a shopping center). One study showed that a 90-minute walk reduced neural activity in an area of the brain linked to risk for mental illness—and lowered levels of rumination.

_____

_____

_____

_____

_____

_____

_____

_____

_____

_____

_____

_____

_____

_____

_____

Choose One to Resolve

From your previous list, choose one scenario to work through and resolve. Don't worry about choosing the "right" one or the "most important" one. You can repeat the four steps to handle worry for each scenario:

1. Express your anger and disappointment.

2. Evaluate your feelings.

3. Brainstorm ideas.

4. Check the facts.

Use your own version of these steps, which you wrote down on page 29, to work through a scenario here.

_____

_____

_____

_____

_____

_____

_____

_____

_____

_____

_____

_____

_____

_____

Rerun the Scene in Your Imagination

As though you were watching a movie in your mind, play the original scene that is troubling you. I had replayed my failed marriage over and over, often making myself right and him wrong, but here I had to really pay attention and get very specific.

Let the scene run all the way through to the unsatisfying conclusion, then write it down here.

_____

_____

_____

_____

_____

_____

_____

_____

_____

_____

_____

_____

_____

_____

_____

QUICK CALM

Try the 4-7-8 breathing technique, known as the "relaxing breath" popularized by Dr. Andrew Weil: quietly breathe in through your nose for 4 seconds, hold the breath for 7 seconds, then exhale forcefully through your mouth for 8 seconds. Repeat the cycle three more times. This mindful breathing can activate the parasympathetic nervous system, giving your anxious brain something else to focus on, and calm your body almost instantly.

Change the Scene

Still in your imagination, replay the scene several times, changing it each time, to prove you can change your thinking. This is where I began to learn that I could change my thoughts. I had a number of scenes, arguments, and frustrated moments from my first marriage to replay. When I changed them, it was very empowering. You, too, can change what you say or do in the scene, or even change what someone else does. Actually, as you change what you do, the other person would have to respond differently to your new behavior in the scene. You can also change the setting if it will make you feel safer. I often suggest to my clients who are struggling with scary scenes that they add a helpful superhero(ine), a caring friend or family member who offers comfort or safety, the police, guardian angels, or other religious figures to provide safety.

Write your new thoughts here.

_____

_____

_____

_____

_____

_____

_____

_____

_____

_____

_____

_____

_____

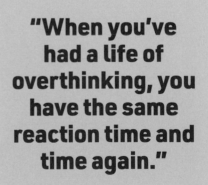

"When you've had a life of overthinking, you have the same reaction time and time again."

—Joel Annesley, life coach

Replay as Much as You Want

Go over the scene until you feel satisfied about the changes you've made. Changing a scene like this gives you some options about what you could do differently in the future. I learned a lot about the mistakes I made and got some ideas about what I'd do differently, such as standing up for myself, and not believing obvious lies.

Write your best new options here.

_____

_____

_____

_____

_____

_____

_____

_____

_____

_____

_____

_____

_____

_____

_____

_____

_____

_____

Change the Other Circumstances

In real life, we can't change what has happened, but in our imagination, we can. If your scene involves someone saying something you don't like, change their words and make them say something more acceptable; or change them into another person (like a beloved grandparent or dear friend) and have them speak as that kind person. For me, this is where I realized my ex-husband looked and sounded like my dad, but wasn't the good man my dad was. Or change the setting, maybe from private to public, or the other way around.

What did you change? How did it feel?

Try Another Scene

Go back to your list from page 46, choose another scene, and repeat the prompts.

Write your scene here.

_____

_____

_____

_____

_____

_____

_____

_____

_____

_____

_____

_____

_____

_____

_____

_____

_____

_____

_____

_____

_____

_____

_____

_____

_____

_____

_____

_____

_____

_____

_____

How do you feel about your power to change your mind?

_____

_____

_____

_____

_____

_____

_____

_____

_____

_____

_____

_____

A Quick Review

Having a list of what you did to reframe your troubling scenarios is useful for when you need to do this exercise again.

Make a brief list of the steps you used, for when you want to use them again.

_____

_____

_____

_____

_____

_____

QUICK CALM

In aromatherapy, lavender is a stress-relieving superstar, along with chamomile, citrus, bergamot, rose, cedarwood, and ylang-ylang. Try them in candles, teas, bubble baths, lotions, eye masks, or diffusers.

_____

_____

_____

_____

_____

Reclaim Your Power

Congratulate yourself on reclaiming power over your thoughts. I was so relieved to have more power in the scene, I called my dearest friend, and she congratulated me and helped me celebrate.

Congratulate yourself here.

_____

_____

_____

_____

_____

_____

_____

_____

_____

_____

_____

_____

_____

_____

_____

_____

_____

> **"Rule number one is, don't sweat the small stuff. Rule number two is, it's all small stuff."**
>
> —Robert Eliot, MD, cardiologist and author of _Is It Worth Dying For?_

Notes

"Perfectionism is the voice of the oppressor."

—Anne Lamott, inspirational author

4. STOP PERFECTIONISM

Perfectionism is a specific kind of worry: being anxious that you must be perfect and that you won't live up to your own standards of perfection. This type of thinking is often the result of growing up around a perfectionist, which means the standards might not even be yours: instead, they're learned behavior. Or perfectionism can be the result of surviving a trauma, as seeking perfection can be an attempt to control life when it's become out of control. This chapter focuses on helping you overcome the things that influence you to be a perfectionist.

▶ If you're struggling with perfectionism, you're not alone. We live in the Age of Information, and we are constantly exposed to images, videos, and articles showing people doing extraordinary and often dangerous things. This inundation of images and information can influence us to believe we should be doing similar things at the same level. Because of this, perfectionism among young people has increased significantly during the past few decades. In fact, data collected on more than 40,000 college students in the United Kingdom, the United States, and Canada between 1989 and 2016 showed that perfectionism was on the rise, leading researchers to suggest that perfectionism may be to blame for this age group's increasing rates of anxiety and depression.

There are certain endeavors, like brain surgery, rocket science, Olympic sports, medicine, the arts, and demanding skills such as performance-level dance and doing magic, for which near-perfection is required. Keep in mind that those pursuits that require precision come with lots of training, as well as lots of safeguards and protections. But that is different from the generalized perfectionism that has you throwing out a perfectly good batch of cupcakes because they're a little crooked or perfection that has paralyzed you when you're trying to do a project for work. In order to be able to write books, I had to let go of the idea of doing it perfectly and remember there are multiple edits where I can get things right; I had to learn to allow myself to write near-gibberish to get down an idea that's difficult to express, and then come back and reorder it later. With the help of the following prompts, you'll learn to understand what perfectionism is, how it works in your life, and what you can do about it.

Understanding Personal Perfectionism

Start by understanding how you pressure yourself to be perfect. Listen to what you say to yourself about not doing something well enough. Consider projects you either couldn't complete or were tense about as you were doing them. You need to understand where the pressure is to correct it.

What do you realize you have trouble doing because you're worried that either you won't be good at it or the result won't be good enough? And whose standards of "good enough" are you judging yourself by?

_____

_____

_____

_____

_____

_____

_____

_____

_____

_____

Perfectionism Impedes Progress

Way back in 1982, when I got my first solo book contract, I was so overwhelmed by the idea of writing a book on my own that I couldn't even read the contract for a few days, until I calmed myself down. I was worried that I couldn't write a good enough book without my previous coauthor, Riley K. Smith.

Are there things you have stopped doing because you felt the outcomes weren't good enough or you felt you weren't good enough at them? Write them here, along with what you were afraid of.

_____

_____

86 percent of workers believe perfectionism impacts their work.

Perfectionism and Avoidance Are Connected

When you feel overwhelmed by something you think you're not going to do well enough, the first impulse is usually to avoid it, like I did by not reading that book contract.

Is there something you'd like to do but won't try? If so, why not?

_____

_____

_____

_____

_____

_____

_____

_____

_____

_____

_____

_____

_____

One-third of employees are considering leaving their workplace because of perfectionist expectations.

_____

_____

_____

_____

_____

_____

Beginner vs. Expert

When we're very young, we know we're beginners, and we usually can allow ourselves to be tentative and inexpert. Toddlers try to walk, fall down, and just get up and try again without worrying about it. But if, perhaps in school or from concerned parents, we get pressured to "do it right" or "get good grades," we can start expecting ourselves to be excellent at everything, even things that are new to us. We might start to compare ourselves to others who have a lot more experience and become competitive with them, as opposed to learning from them.

Are you comparing your beginner work to that of an expert?
Write the critical things you're saying about what you've done
or not done and whether you've done it badly or well.

_____

_____

_____

_____

_____

_____

_____

68 percent of workers believe perfectionism leads to burnout.

_____

_____

_____

_____

_____

The Power of Self-Criticism

Criticism from others has to get past your critical thinking skills to hurt, but criticism from yourself hits you deeply.

Are you more afraid of others' criticism or your own?
Who is your worst critic?

_____

_____

_____

_____

A Canadian study showed that adults over age 65 who placed high expectations on themselves to be perfect had a 51 percent increased risk of death; if, however, they had a chronic condition— say, diabetes, where meticulous attention to detail can be lifesaving— that figure was 26 percent _lower_ risk of death.

Find Your Kindness

Most of us understand how to be encouraging to a friend or family member who is struggling, but we often have a hard time being encouraging to ourselves.

How would you behave toward and talk to another person you care about when it comes to getting something done?

_____

_____

_____

_____

_____

_____

_____

_____

_____

_____

_____

_____

_____

_____

_____

_____

72 percent of workers believe perfectionism is harmful to building relationships.

Turn Kindness Inward

You can learn to direct the same sort of encouragement and support that you've given to people you care about toward yourself.

Write something encouraging and kind to yourself about what you've been doing about these projects that you're worried you won't be good enough at.

_____

_____

_____

_____

About 88 percent of gifted adolescents self-identify as having perfectionistic tendencies.

_____

_____

_____

_____

_____

_____

_____

_____

_____

_____

_____

_____

_____

Permit Yourself to Learn

When you understand that becoming expert at anything requires starting at the beginning and not being familiar with it at first, you can open yourself up to learning and be tolerant of mistakes. Instead of seeing others as competition for who is the best, you can relax and learn from them.

If you think of yourself as a beginner and approach the things in the questions on pages 62 and 63 in a way that takes it slow and makes it easier, how does it change your approach?

_____

_____

_____

_____

_____

_____

_____

_____

_____

_____

_____

_____

_____

_____

_____

_____

66 percent of workers believe perfectionism leads to fear of failure and conflict avoidance.

Take a New Look

If you have what Zen masters call *Shoshin*, "a beginner's mind," you have an attitude of openness, eagerness, and a lack of preconceptions when studying, even at an advanced level, just as a beginner would. The term was popularized outside of Japan by Shunryū Suzuki's 1970 book *Zen Mind, Beginner's Mind*. Approaching tasks, even familiar ones, as though they're brand new to you frees you from having to be an expert and can open you to new ideas and new ways of thinking about familiar things.

Look at a task or event as though you've never done it before. How different does the project look to you when you have smaller expectations because you're a beginner?

66 percent of workplaces struggle with perfectionism.

Give Yourself Permission

You have the greatest authority over yourself, if you use it. When you give yourself permission to do something, and to correct your mistakes (any mistake deserves a retake), you'll find the obstacles that come from outside sources disappear.

Write ten times, "I, (your name), always do the best I can, and I do it well. If I make a mistake, I can correct it." After you've done that, write about how it feels. Does it change your approach?

_____

_____

_____

_____

_____

_____

_____

_____

_____

_____

_____

_____

_____

_____

_____

_____

_____

_____

Notes

"Obsession is the single most wasteful human activity, because with an obsession you keep coming back and back and back to the same question and never get an answer."

—Norman Mailer, American novelist

5. STOP OBSESSIVE THINKING

Obsessive thinking is like perseveration, but more intense. You think the same thoughts over and over, and your mind can't focus on anything else. Obsessive thinking can be paralyzing, stopping you from functioning mentally. The obsessive thoughts can sometimes create obsessive behaviors, like counting or uncontrollable handwashing. When obsession becomes compulsion, you feel you have no choice but to act on the obsession. (Most people with this problem, however, are just obsessing, not acting.)

▶ A number of my clients have been troubled by obsessive thoughts, which often are masked as anxious feelings. The thoughts have spawned fascinating habits, like baking endless cookies or cupcakes that no one will eat, frantically cleaning or repairing things, and a lot of counting, like counting every step while doing a chore or counting fence posts or sidewalk squares while walking. Obsessive thoughts can also spawn addictions like drinking, gambling, or overspending to escape the pressure.

Keep in mind that your thoughts belong to you, and you can change them. You alone decide if you're "good enough" and if you're okay with you. It's helpful to note that you can't just ignore an obsessive thought. To get rid of it, you have to replace it, which is what we'll do here.

Recognize Obsessive Thoughts

If there's any thought you're dwelling on so much that you can't get rid of it, consider that an obsessive thought. Some people obsess about what others think, about aging and appearance, about not being loveable, about something left undone or something you need to do in the future that you're worried about. If you grew up in a strict religious or military home, or with any kind of super-demanding parent, you're likely to obsess about being inadequate in some way.

What recurring, intrusive thoughts have you had?

_____

_____

_____

_____

_____

_____

_____

_____

_____

_____

_____

_____

_____

_____

_____

_____

Identify How These Thoughts Affect Your Life

Obsessive thoughts are always negative. It's like having a nagging, demanding parent in your own head, following you around and carping about whatever you're doing. This creates anxiety and interferes with your productivity and relaxation.

How do these repetitive thoughts obstruct your daily activities?

_____

_____

_____

_____

_____

_____

_____

_____

_____

_____

_____

_____

_____

_____

_____

_____

_____

_____

_____

_____

_____

Obsessive Thoughts Create Obsessive Actions

Think about where your thoughts are accompanied by repetitive actions (nail biting, scratching, or picking), counting things you don't need to count (sidewalk lines or fence posts), or superstitious behaviors (like repetitively checking the doors and windows).

Do you notice you're doing any obsessive actions? What are they?

Obsessive-compulsive disorder (OCD) affects about 1 percent of the U.S. population, with women three times more likely than men to have the condition

What Gets Your Attention?

Although the thoughts beget the actions, the actions may be the first thing you notice. For example, I was a nail biter as a child, and now I notice when I'm paying excessive attention to my nails, which is my clue that I'm worried about something. Then I can track down and correct the worry. You may notice that you're thinking endlessly and not productively about something, so the thoughts get your attention first.

What do you notice first, the thoughts or the actions?
How do you know you're being obsessive?

_____

_____

_____

_____

_____

_____

_____

_____

_____

_____

_____

_____

_____

_____

_____

In a study across six continents, researchers found that 94 percent of participants experienced at least one unwanted or intrusive thought in the previous three months. This means they happen to almost everyone from time to time.

Focus on Your Obsessive Thoughts

Instead of trying to push away the thoughts or masking them with actions, focus on them. What are your obsessive thoughts? For most of my clients, these are scary thoughts like "What if..." or "Everyone hates me," or "I'm broken/worthless/unlovable." As I noted earlier, my fears of poverty produced a frightening "bag lady" image I was frequently troubled by.

Write or describe your obsessive thoughts here.

_____

_____

_____

_____

_____

_____

_____

_____

Post-traumatic stress disorder (PTSD) affects nearly 4 percent of the U.S. population, involving women five times more than men. Like OCD, it is closely related to anxiety disorders.

Counter the Negative Thoughts

Once you get clear enough on the troublesome thoughts, they usually seem less scary or clearly false. They might come from nasty things other people, such as classmates when you were in school, have said to you. For each thought on the previous page, write a kinder counterthought. For example: for the thought "I'm broken," you could write, "I'm human and not perfect, but I'm OK." For "Nobody can love me," write down, "I love myself, and when others feel that love, they love me too." For my bag-lady thoughts, I wrote, "I am financially OK. I can earn the money I need."

Write down a counterthought for each thought on the previous page.

Create Affirmations

Take the counterthoughts to your most troubling thoughts and make affirmations out of them. For example, if we use "I'm human and not perfect, but I'm OK," we would write it here like this: "I, (your name), am a normal human, and I'm not perfect, but I'm perfectly good enough." You can write an affirmation to counter each obsessive thought. (I wrote, "I, Tina, am financially OK, and I can earn the money I need.") Many of my clients share this with a close, trusted friend or family member to get another opinion on whether the counterthought is kind enough; you might try the same.

Write your affirmations here.

Repetition is the Cure

Your mind ranks the things you do most often as the most important. To counter negative thoughts you've been thinking for a long time, you need to replace them with more positive thinking. The way to do that is with repetition.

Write one of your affirmations ten times here.

1. _____

2. _____

3. _____

4. _____

5. _____

6. _____

7. _____

8. _____

9. _____

10. _____

How Much Repetition?

Once you have written your affirmation ten times, you should know it by heart. Write it once more here, then promise to say it to yourself morning and night, and any time during the day that you feel the negative, obsessive thought intruding. If you say it often enough, it will overpower the negative thought, and because it's not an anxious thought, it won't be accompanied by the obsessive feelings. Whether you are Christian or not, it's helpful to know that Jesus commanded forgiveness. Matthew 18: 21–22 reads, "Then Peter came up and said to him, 'Lord, how often will my brother sin against me, and I forgive him? As many as seven times?' Jesus said to him, 'I do not say to you seven times, but seventy-seven times.'"

When I do affirmations, I repeat them ten times each, over a period of at least eight days, which usually seems to be enough. Consider what Lewis B. Smedes wrote in *Forgive and Forget*: "To forgive is to set a prisoner free and discover that the prisoner was you." Find out how many repetitions cures your repetitive negative thinking.

Rewrite your affirmations here.

_____

_____

_____

_____

_____

_____

_____

_____

_____

_____

_____

You've Conquered Obsessive Thinking

Congratulate yourself on having learned how to conquer obsessive thinking here. Write: "I, (your name), have learned how to overcome my negative thoughts with counterthoughts. I can use my counterthoughts any time the negative thoughts trouble me."

Congratulate yourself here.

_____

_____

_____

_____

_____

_____

_____

_____

_____

_____

_____

_____

_____

_____

_____

_____

_____

_____

_____

Notes

"When fear makes your choices for you, no security measures on earth will keep the things you dread from finding you."

—Martha Beck, author

6. STOP AVOIDANCE

Avoidance is thinking a lot of random thoughts to avoid feeling or thinking about something unpleasant. It is a major component of Post-Traumatic Stress (PTS) because the feelings associated with trauma can be overwhelming.

▶ The main problem with avoidance is that it sets up a fight between your psyche, which wants to express and explore the traumatic event and associated feelings, and the urge to avoid focusing on those things, which leaves your mind in turmoil.

Identify Avoidance Behavior

Avoidance behaviors can include sleeping too much, posting on social media, texting, talking on the phone, playing games instead of getting things done, eating too much, zoning out in front of the TV or bingeing on streaming shows, even doing a hobby rather than what you're supposed to be doing. Drinking or eating too much is also often an avoidance behavior.

Identify your avoidance behaviors here.

_____

_____

_____

_____

_____

_____

_____

There are healthy forms of avoidance or escape behavior: applying sunscreen to avoid sunburn, using an oven mitt to avoid burning yourself, strapping a baby into a stroller to avoid them falling out, etc. All are reasonable and not problematic.

What Are You Avoiding?

When you find yourself engaging in avoidance behaviors, think about what you are avoiding. For most people, it's either something scary or something you don't want to do but think you must do. For me, it was fear of poverty and being alone in the world. My escape was to be constantly busy. Another example might be having a work (or class) assignment, but hating your job (or the class), so you avoid doing the assignment. Or being in a car accident then avoiding driving by getting busy at home. Or having a painful breakup, so you wind up cleaning your refrigerator instead of going to a party where you might meet someone attractive.

What are you avoiding with your behaviors?

Avoidance Never Works for Long

At first, avoiding what troubles you can feel good and can take the pressure off. But avoidance creates its own kind of pressure, and after a while, you'll feel trapped and stifled by it. For example, if you stay home because you're worried about what people will think, you could eventually develop agoraphobia, the fear of going out or trying anything new, and then you'd be truly trapped. Other kinds of avoidance can irritate or hurt those around you, who constantly feel disappointed and let down by you. Of course, avoiding getting things done at work or school can have terrible consequences, and avoiding criticism can cause you to become a recluse or a frantic people pleaser.

Whatever it is you're trying to avoid, how well has that worked for you? Did it go away? Are you ready to try something that works?

_____

_____

_____

_____

_____

_____

_____

_____

_____

_____

_____

_____

_____

Face the Relationship Demons

Face your demons. Maybe what you've been (unsuccessfully) trying to avoid has to do with relationships: a current relationship that's not working, no matter how hard you try; a family relationship that's difficult and maybe painful; a friendship that feels too one-sided; a relationship from your past that was traumatic; or maybe it's your relationship with yourself that's not working as well as you'd like. By identifying the things that terrify or trouble you, you take back your power from them.

Name your relationship demons here.

Identify the Activity Demons

Inner demons can also be activity related: Maybe your work isn't satisfying, but you feel trapped; or maybe you're working at something because somebody else wants you to. This is often true of legacy careers: your parents expect you to follow in the family footsteps and be a lawyer or a doctor, or you come from a military family and are expected to enlist. Maybe there's something you would like to do, like art or music, but have been told it's too hard. Maybe you're struggling with the shoulds: I should exercise, go to school, make something of myself, lose weight.

Write your activity demons here.

Pin Down the Expectation Demons

Demons can also be expectations you have of yourself that don't really match who you are or your abilities. They sound like, "I'm too fat; I should diet or exercise." Or, "My house is dirty; I should keep it perfectly clean." Or, maybe you're haunted by things you expect of others that they are not interested in, such as, "My son needs a wife," or, "My sister should have a better job."

Write your expectation demons here.

_____

_____

_____

_____

_____

_____

_____

_____

_____

_____

_____

_____

_____

_____

_____

_____

_____

QUICK CALM

Yoga, meditation, getting a massage or pedicure, journaling, and napping are all ways to exercise your mind and spirit. They might not be instantly calming when you're anxious, but you'll feel better when you're done.

Time to Face the Demons

Whatever demons you have identified, it's time to face them. Choose one, and write what you want to say to it, face to face. Get all your frustrations and feelings out. Express your anger, your fear, your sadness, and whatever is troubling you.

Write your dialogue with your demons here.

_____

_____

_____

_____

_____

_____

_____

_____

_____

_____

_____

QUICK CALM

Studies show that the methodical act of chewing gum keeps blood flowing to the brain. You can concentrate better and keep your head level during a bout of anxiety. (And it just might keep you from stress eating.)

Repeat for All the Demons

Repeat that last step from page 96 for each of your demons. Take your time and use more paper than you have here, if you need it.

_____

_____

_____

_____

_____

_____

_____

_____

_____

_____

_____

_____

_____

_____

_____

_____

_____

_____

_____

_____

QUICK CALM

If you tend to have anxious thoughts, consider keeping a centering object on hand, whether that's a smooth "worry stone" or stress ball, a meaningful piece of jewelry or knickknack, even a small stuffed animal or fidget spinner. When the thoughts arise, you can focus on and touch that object; if it's not near you when the thoughts arise, think about touching it later on, keeping a clear picture of how it feels in your mind.

Turn Your Demons into Helpers

Now, assume your demons want to help you, but are misguided as to how to do it. Tell each demon what they can do that would actually be helpful. For example, when you feel badgered and pushed, that demon is actually your own mind trying to motivate you, but it's going about it the wrong way. If you feel frightened about or stymied by something, maybe that demon is trying to get your attention and move you in a different direction. If you feel frustrated, perhaps that demon is telling you that it's time to change something or go about it in a new way. If your demon is yourself, tell yourself what you need from you. For example, "I know you're trying to motivate me, but fear and pressure do the opposite. If you want to motivate me, encourage me." Then practice turning your scary or pressuring thought into a motivating one.

Write your instructions to the demons for what would really help you here.

_____

_____

_____

_____

_____

_____

_____

_____

_____

_____

_____

_____

_____

Repeat for All Demons

Depending on how beset by demons you feel, it may take several passes through these prompts to confront all of them. Start with one that feels difficult, and work with it until you achieve a better working relationship. Then go on to another one.

QUICK CALM

Drop your shoulders! Take a moment to feel where your shoulders are—they tend to rise when we're tense. Sit up straight, take a few deep breaths, and concentrate on lowering your shoulder blades down your back.

Notes

"The art of pleasing is the art of deception."

—Luc de Clapiers, marquis de Vauvenargues

7. STOP PEOPLE PLEASING

People pleasing is a less-recognized kind of obsessive thinking, when you're fixated on what other people think about you or what they want from you. Your day is spent focusing on what others say (or your guesses about what they are thinking) so that you don't know your own opinion. You may have grown up focused on a dominant parent, or you've been taught people pleasing by another people pleaser: for example, a mom who constantly worries about what the neighbors or her family would think about something or a passive parent who is focused on pleasing a dominant parent. You need to learn to form your own opinions and not put too much focus on what others will think or want you to do.

▶ While we all enjoy making other people happy, and pleasing them to a degree, if it runs your life, and you are not at the top of the list of the people you are pleasing, you risk developing Impostor Syndrome, where you don't feel as though you're really yourself. You feel as though you're acting a part rather than being yourself. These prompts will help you to put yourself front and center.

may be how you look and dress; what you do for work or hobbies; copying how others look, or what they do or say (like celebrities or media influencers); how you keep your house or what you cook; owning flashy cars or jewelry; or what you choose to say or post on social media. Other people-pleasing attitudes might include apologizing all the time, agreeing with everyone, deferring your own needs to meet others', feeling responsible for how someone else feels, avoiding conflict, an inability to say no or to establish boundaries and just accepting what other people do or say (even if it's rude, nasty, or inconsiderate).

What do you do to please others? Be as specific as you can.

_____

_____

_____

_____

_____

_____

_____

_____

_____

_____

_____

_____

_____

_____

_____

_____

_____

Review the List

A lot of people-pleasing behavior and thought begins so early in life that we just accept it, and we don't really know what our own opinion is. Reviewing the list, thinking about whether it's what *you* want to do, can help you let go of people pleasing.

Go over the list, and for each item, ask yourself what you think about it. Would you do it differently if you were just pleasing yourself (and, if so, how)?

_____

_____

_____

_____

_____

_____

_____

_____

_____

_____

_____

_____

_____

_____

_____

_____

_____

Ask Your Own Opinion

Practice asking your own opinion about several things today. For example, as you're getting dressed, ask yourself what you'd like to focus on today, and what's important to you. Consider what you're choosing to wear and whether it's truly your choice. What color do you enjoy wearing? Or what textures and lines? Or consider what you're planning to do, and ask yourself if you want to do that. Sometimes we need to do things that are not our favorite, but we should at least know the difference between something we need to do and something we're doing to please someone else.

Write your answers here.

Consider Your Personal Space

Even if you have only one room to call your own, it can reflect who you are. Take a look at your home. Move from space to space and really look at it. Does it please you? Does it reflect who you are? Does it suit your taste? Does it befit your lifestyle? Are your favorite colors here? Are there photos or art depicting your preferences? Is there anything you'd like to change? What do you think someone visiting your home for the first time would learn about you? Is that what you'd want them to learn?

Write your answers here.

_____

_____

_____

_____

_____

_____

_____

_____

_____

_____

_____

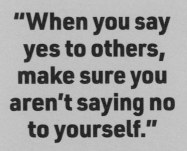

_____

_____

"When you say yes to others, make sure you aren't saying no to yourself."

—Paulo Coelho, novelist

_____

_____

_____

What's Your Style?

When I was young, I felt very confused about how to dress. In high school, I dressed like my classmates, but as a young adult I felt lost. Since my mom didn't really have style, a friend took me to a clothing store and asked me to tell her what I liked and didn't like. She reflected my answers back to me. It was then that I learned what colors I preferred, that textures were important to me, and how to choose them. Look at yourself in the mirror and try to be as objective and noncritical as you can. Are you dressed in a way that's comfortable for you? Are you wearing colors and styles you like? Does how you dress tell other people something about who you are? Is that what you'd want them to think? Even if you have a dress code for work (uniform or suits/dresses), you can express your own style in accessories or colors.

Write your answers here.

_____

_____

_____

_____

_____

_____

_____

_____

_____

_____

_____

_____

_____

_____

What Would You Like to Change?

After considering what you think about your day, your home, and how you're dressed, is there anything you'd really like to change? For example, you're tired of wearing high heels at the office, when what you really want to wear are flats or running shoes. (You can keep a pair of neutral heels in your drawer, should a specific meeting demand them.) Or, tired of suits and ties, maybe you can wear a cardigan and keep a jacket and tie on hand for when needed. Or, if you're sick of your bland, hand-me-down furniture, and you don't want to (or can't) buy new stuff, you might want to cover it with a throw or pillows or buy just one thing that adds a pop of color to your living room.

Write your changes here.

_____

_____

_____

_____

_____

_____

_____

_____

_____

_____

_____

A study from Lancaster University in the U.K. showed that as social media users became stressed by what they saw, they switched to different activities like chatting with friends, scrolling newsfeeds, and posting updates. This behavior kept them on the platform longer and increased their risk of becoming addicted to it.

_____

_____

_____

_____

What Changes Can You Make?

Considering your situation, your budget, and what's within your means, what changes can you make to reflect more of who you are in your plans and surroundings? You have a lot of choices, even if your budget is limited. (Thrift stores and consignment shops are great for furniture and clothing. Maybe you can add some colorful throw pillows to that bland furniture or find some ballet flats on the cheap.) Painting furniture is another inexpensive way to reflect your own taste.

Write your proposed changes here.

_____

_____

_____

_____

_____

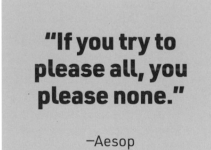

"If you try to please all, you please none."

—Aesop

_____

_____

_____

_____

You Can Choose What You Want

How you look, where you live, and all your choices could be about you and what you like. Once you know those things, you'll be much more able to communicate your preferences to others and cooperate with them if you're doing something together, like sharing a living space. When a roommate and I moved in together, we put all our decorative objects, framed prints, etc. in one room, and then each of us selected something from the other's pile to place in the home. We kept taking turns until all rooms were decorated. Our bedroom styles were our own personal choice. This is what healthy compromise, as opposed to people pleasing, looks like.

Recap what you've learned here.

_____

_____

_____

_____

_____

_____

_____

_____

_____

_____

_____

_____

_____

_____

_____

_____

Consider Your Activities in the Same Light

Now broaden your focus to include activities you like, whether you're an adventurer or a homebody or some combination of those, your dreams of travel or dreams of accomplishment, and anything else you'd like to focus on, to learn more about who you are and your own preferences. Even if you're reading, watching TV, on social media, or listening to a podcast, create a habit of pausing and asking yourself what you think about what you're absorbing. Ask yourself who you admire and why. Pretend you're part of the show, and contribute your own thoughts.

Write your discoveries here. There are no wrong answers.

_____

_____

_____

_____

_____

_____

A study out of Northwestern University on coping pattern differences between men and women found that more women (54 percent) exhibited people-pleasing behavior than men (40 percent).

Review Your Choices

This is a big topic. Review the questions in this section, and consider how your point of view has changed. While it's important to be able to get along with others, it's equally important to honor who you are and to know your preferences, even when they don't fit the "norm."

Write your conclusions here.

_____

_____

_____

_____

_____

_____

_____

_____

_____

> **"Care about what other people think and you will always be their prisoner."**
>
> —Lao Tzu,
> Chinese philosopher

_____

_____

_____

_____

_____

_____

_____

_____

_____

_____

Notes

> **"You wouldn't worry so much about what others think of you if you realized how seldom they do."**
>
> —Olin Miller, American writer and humorist

"If you don't believe in yourself, somewhere or another, you sabotage yourself."

—Jason Day, professional golfer

8. STOP SELF-SABOTAGE

Call it shooting yourself in the foot. Getting in your own way. Being your own worst enemy. Self-sabotage is having constant negative thoughts about yourself and what you're doing. It's constantly predicting a negative outcome of whatever you're trying to accomplish. Self-sabotage can lead to the unwillingness to do anything because it's no use, it won't work, or you're not worth it. None of these thoughts are true, but they may seem true to you. The work of this chapter will be to root out your self-sabotage and counteract it.

▶ We all walk around with a constant inner dialogue, talking to ourselves. Some of the dialogue is about the day-to-day: what I have to do today, what I'm concerned about, how I'm going to handle things. But the rest of it we picked up early in life, and it tends to be pretty negative. As young children, we are emotionally vulnerable and take criticism very seriously, and often it turns into a negative dialogue directed at the self: "I shouldn't have done that; I'm such an idiot." "No one will like me in this new place." "I'm not doing it right." "I'm stupid, lazy, incompetent, or just plain wrong." As my dear friend and coauthor Riley K. Smith used to say, "Wrong, wrong, wrongy-wrong wrong." If you experience a traumatic event, then self-blame for the event becomes internalized as Post-Traumatic Stress and added to your negative self-talk.

Become Aware of Negative Feelings about Yourself

Even if you're unaware of it, you're statistically likely to have a running critical commentary going on. You're getting used to focusing on your own thoughts by now and discovering what they are. Use that new skill to pin down your negative thoughts and focus on them, so you can better understand what you want to change about them.

What are the negative feelings you have about yourself?

_____

_____

_____

_____

_____

> **"Unless we have constant witnesses to our hard work, we are convinced we pull off every day of our lives through smoke and mirrors."**
>
> —Sarah Breathnach,
> *Peace and Plenty*

Pinpoint Where the Negative Self-Talk Came From

You were not born feeling negative about yourself. You learned the negative ideas and feelings somewhere. Who did you learn them from? For example, I had a lot of negative feelings about being female, yet my beloved dad had treated me as if I were his only son, teaching me that I could do anything he could do. Since the negative feelings were at cross-purposes with what he taught me, they had to come from somewhere else: society. When I found the early feminism movement, I learned to think more positively about being female. And I realized that society's prejudices didn't have to limit me.

Where do you think your negative feelings of self might have come from?

Mistaken Beliefs from Well-Intentioned Adults

We're often negatively influenced by well-meaning but misguided family members who criticize us under the guise of trying to motivate us. Even though they love us, they can be wrong about us. We also get negative influences from school, church, our surroundings (like neighborhoods), and the society at large. Upon reflection, we might realize that these influencers had the wrong idea. For example, you might have been told that "boys don't cry" or you should have a "stiff upper lip," and you now find that you prefer to be free and honest with your emotions, whatever they may be. Any thoughts beginning with "boys/men or girls/women should…." are ideas you gleaned from elsewhere, and they may not really apply to you; even gender assignment can be imposed on you. You are an individual, not a representative of some collective idea like gender, race, ethnicity, etc.

What did you come to believe about yourself that you now know is not true?

_____

_____

_____

_____

_____

_____

_____

_____

_____

_____

_____

_____

_____

_____

Overcoming What You Were Told

Oddly enough, when we limit ourselves by trying to "overcome" what we have been told is negative, we are still trying to please outside forces; it usually backfires because people will reflect your own views of yourself back at you. For example, if you feel that you're not good at interacting with people, you'll find people call you "shy" and "awkward." That's not true; they're just reflecting back what you believe about yourself. What's true is that you have social preferences, and they might be less group oriented. It can feel worse if you are a member of a marginalized community or identify in a way the culture around you seems to have a problem with. I used to be called "odd" and "different" a lot, mostly because my father raised me to think for myself, and I asked a lot of inconvenient questions. I eventually decided I liked being different, and what people said stopped feeling bad to me. When I met my best friend at a job, she said to me, "You're the weirdest person I ever met." I responded, "Thank you," and we've been close friends since 1968.

What negative beliefs about yourself have other people "confirmed" for you?

_____

_____

_____

_____

_____

_____

_____

_____

_____

_____

_____

_____

_____

How You See Yourself

When you look at yourself as objectively as you can and consider what you think of you, rather than what other people have told you, you will probably find that there's a big difference between what you're told and what you really think.

How do those negative beliefs contrast with how you see yourself? Do you see yourself the way they see you?

_____

_____

_____

_____

_____

_____

_____

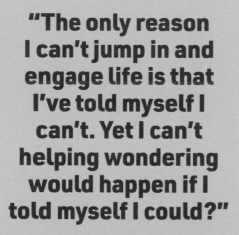

"The only reason I can't jump in and engage life is that I've told myself I can't. Yet I can't helping wondering would happen if I told myself I could?"

—Craig D. Lounsbrough, author and counselor

Reframe Negative Thinking

You can reframe negative beliefs into positive ones. For example, if they call you "shy," you can reframe that to be "introspective," "thoughtful," "comfortable by yourself," or "low-key." Not everyone has to be the life of the party. Some of the world's best thinkers, like Henry David Thoreau, Albert Einstein, and Edna St. Vincent Millay, were quiet, self-contained people. Most innovation comes from "outliers" or people who don't fit the majority culture. Outsiders often see the problem more clearly.

Using the list of your so-called "natural" traits, reframe the negative beliefs about yourself into positive ones.

_____

_____

_____

_____

_____

_____

_____

_____

_____

_____

_____

_____

_____

_____

_____

_____

_____

_____

Introduce Your New Positive Identity

Use your reframed beliefs about yourself to write an introduction to the world about yourself: For example, I might write: "This is Tina: She's friendly but prefers people one at a time. She loves her friends, she's smart, and she enjoys playing within her mind. She'd rather read than listen to podcasts or music. She's a loyal friend. She loves animals." Or, if you're outgoing, you can say "This is (your name). He/she/they love to party, enjoy groups of friends, and being spontaneous."

Write your introduction here. Edit it until you feel really good about it.

QUICK CALM

Just 10 minutes of petting a dog or cat can reduce stress hormones and promote a calm feeling.

Repeat and Share Your New Identity

Repeat this new positive description of yourself to yourself several times. Share it with a few supportive friends or family members. Keep it handy for whenever the old, negative beliefs emerge. If a new negative belief surfaces, rewrite it as you did on page 125.

How are you feeling about yourself now? Is this a change from how you felt before?

_____

_____

_____

_____

_____

_____

_____

_____

_____

_____

_____

_____

_____

_____

_____

_____

_____

_____

_____

_____

Where Will Your New Definition of Yourself Lead?

Having a new, positive identity will cause you to see your life differently. You may want to act on some of these differences, especially if you think through how your new identity, your new self, will approach your life. Understanding who you are can motivate you to change what you do.

With this new feeling about yourself, is there anything about your life you'd like to change? Is there anything you're doing now that you'd like to do differently?

Counter Negativity from Others

Armed with your new, positive image of yourself, you can now recognize negativity that comes at you as being a problem for the persons who perceive you that way, not for you. A dear friend of mine, an African American woman who earned the title "Mrs. America," was doing some of the resulting publicity tours, and when she was in Georgia, a woman asked her, "Are you Mrs. Africa?" My friend answered, "Mrs. America: you know, land of the brave, home of the free." With that, she reframed the whole encounter and asserted her power in a humorous, but effective, way.

When people say things that cause you to feel badly about yourself, how will you counter them with the positive interpretation? Use your reframed list from page 125 and your introduction from page 126 to work through negative things others say on occasion, then figure out an effective, reframing response to each one.

_____

_____

_____

_____

_____

_____

_____

_____

_____

_____

_____

_____

_____

Notes

_____

_____

_____

_____

_____

_____

_____

_____

_____

_____

_____

_____

> **"The underbelly of the human psyche, what is often referred to as our dark side, is the origin of every act of self-sabotage. Birthed out of shame, fear, and denial, it misdirects our good intentions and drives us to unthinkable acts of self-destruction and not-so-unbelievable acts of self sabotage."**
>
> —Debbie Ford, author and lecturer

"The best things happen when you're not overthinking it."

—Ben Zobrist, professional baseball player

9. RESOLVE THE ORIGINS OF OVERTHINKING

Overthinking is the product of your history. Most of it is probably learned: if you grew up with a worrier or a perfectionist, you may have learned to think the way they do. Perhaps you're repeating hurtful things to yourself that were said to you in the past.

▶ Overthinking can also arise from trauma, when something terrible happens and you are fearful that it will happen again, or you're blaming yourself for it. If you were marginalized, judged, teased, bullied, or intimidated, overthinking can be a way of trying to avoid the trauma reoccurring. Understanding where the habit comes from will help you overcome it.

Behavior Clues

There are some telltale clues that indicate you might be acting on learned behavior. If you have trouble with any of the following, you are most likely reacting and responding to learned behavior:

- ▶ procrastination

- ▶ refusing to accept or admit you need help

- ▶ setting goals that are too high or low

- ▶ negative self-talk or criticism

- ▶ making excuses or shifting blame to others

- ▶ picking fights (you're surrounded by lots of conflict and drama)

- ▶ constantly seeking approval

- ▶ not speaking up for yourself

- ▶ overindulging in alcohol, food, shopping, or gambling

- ▶ avoiding people or situations that make you uncomfortable

Which of these clues have you noticed apply to you? List them here because you're going to counteract the underlying learned behavior in this chapter.

_____

_____

_____

_____

_____

_____

_____

_____

Early Onset of Worrying

Worrying can begin as early as age 8, when we are developing rational thought. At that age, we are still striving to please the adults around us, and it's also an age when nightmares develop, as our brains strive to manage all the previously unregistered information about the world around us. Trying for perfection can be a way to create a feeling of safety.

How early do you remember worrying, ruminating, or getting stressed about doing things perfectly? What were some of the things you worried about?

_____

_____

_____

_____

_____

_____

_____

_____

_____

_____

_____

_____

_____

_____

> **"Worrying is like paying a debt you don't owe."**
>
> —Mark Twain, novelist and satirist

Learning Overthinking through Imitation

We often learn the various types of overthinking by imitating someone close to us. In my case, it was my beloved dad. He ran the hotel/bar/restaurant we lived in, he was a worrier, and nothing was ever perfect enough for him. He was loving and kind, but also driven. He had several heart attacks before he died at age 58, and I believe he worried himself to death. He loved me a lot, and I admired him, so I adopted his habits. Many of my clients have had parents who controlled them with guilt or shame, which led to their insecurity and tendencies to overthink.

Who were you around who was a worrier, a perfectionist, a people pleaser, ruminator, etc.?

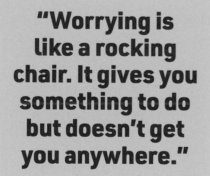

"Worrying is like a rocking chair. It gives you something to do but doesn't get you anywhere."

—Erma Bombeck, author

Adopting Others' Habits

Along with the thinking patterns, we can pick up thinking habits from others. From my dad, I learned to be very exacting and hard on myself. I double-checked everything. This had its good points, like doing well in school, but also its bad side, like not ever feeling satisfied that I had done a good job and not being able to accept a compliment. My clients have taken on family habits like drinking too much, incompetence with finances, dysfunctional relationship habits, and other destructive patterns.

What thinking habits did you learn from the overthinker(s) in your life?

Talk Back to Negative Thinking

My clients often feel liberated when they learn to talk back to their early authority figures. I, too, had to learn to talk back to my negative thinking. For example, I could say to those thoughts (the dad in my head): "Okay, Dad, I've got this, you can relax now." My mom worried about health issues; she came from a family of osteopaths. I can sometimes hear her nattering in my head about what I'm eating or my health status, and I can say, "Mom, I take good care of myself; no need to worry."

How can you counter the negative or obsessive thoughts you learned?

_____

_____

_____

_____

Speak Truth to Negativity

When you counter negative thinking with a truthful and opposite thought, you remove its power over you. Like all changes to thinking, it takes repetition, but it's often surprising how easy it is to conquer negative thinking once you know how. If you're paralyzed by trying to get it perfect, say your counterthoughts out loud: "This is not something I need to do perfectly." For example, in the case of writing this book, I can remind myself that I can come back later and edit what I write. So, while I'd like the book to be as perfect as possible, I don't have to do it alone or all at once.

Say your counterthoughts aloud, then write them here (or on page 144).

_____

_____

_____

_____

_____

Develop a Positive Thinking Habit

Develop a habit of noticing when your thoughts are in your way and then countering them with more positive thoughts. Recognize which thoughts come from someone else, and who it is, and counter them with original thoughts of your own. For example, if your mom was always urging you to eat, or saying you were eating the wrong foods or too much food, allow that to be her opinion and her problem, and don't accept it as yours. You can decide what you want to eat and say to the mom in your head (who may be different from the real-life mom you know), "Mom, this is my choice, not yours. I'm okay; I'm not going to starve."

What learned thinking came from where, and how can you counter it? List each negative-thinking role model, their negative words, and your positive counterthought.

_____

_____

_____

_____

_____

_____

_____

_____

_____

_____

_____

_____

_____

_____

_____

Replace Negative Thinking with Positive Thoughts

Positive thoughts can cancel out negative thoughts. You can also replace problem thinking with more positive thinking. For example, you can recognize that you learned to be worried about what others will think because your mother always was, and decide that it's more important for you to know what you think than what your neighbors think. You could, for example, say to that mom in your head, "Mom, it's more important to me what I think, not what they think, and I'm in charge now."

Write the problem thought here and how you want to counter it.

_____

_____

_____

_____

_____

_____

_____

"I think and think and think. I've thought myself out of happiness one million times, but never once into it."

—Jonathan Safran Foer, American novelist

Negativity from the Environment

Family, culture, religion, school, and other early environments can also be sources of problem thinking. Being bullied at school, learning from a punitive church or school environment, or absorbing societal negativity focused on your ethnicity or culture can also be the source of problem thinking. If you hear, as a child, that there's something wrong with you/your looks/your body, or your culture/gender identity/ethnicity, or if you feel that you don't fit in, you can absorb these attitudes and become prejudiced toward yourself. This can lead to all kinds of problem thinking, worry, fearfulness, and even obsessive negative thoughts about yourself.

Use this space to list the negative things you might have absorbed about yourself from your environment.

_____

_____

_____

_____

_____

_____

_____

_____

_____

_____

_____

_____

_____

_____

_____

Counter Environmental Negativity

Negativity, bigotry, and criticism will continue to exist in the larger culture, so it's important to identify these environmental negative influences and counter them. Then, when you see a commercial, a billboard, or a nasty post on social media, or hear an "expert" saying bigoted statements on TV, you'll already be countering it with your positive thoughts, and it won't sink in. Counter the negative thoughts in the previous step on page 141 with more enlightened thoughts. Realize that people who criticized you are always wrong because they couldn't know you.

Write your enlightened thoughts about your culture, religion, ethnicity, and personal attributes (weight, height, age, attractiveness) here. They can be both negative and positive thoughts. You can criticize and reject some aspects of your culture, family, and religion (meaning, you don't think you want them to apply to you), while enjoying and adapting others.

Keep the Good Messages

It's important to separate the positive messages from the negative ones. You've learned things about yourself, your culture, your family traditions, your ethnicity and origins that were good and that you love. All cultures, races, religions, etc. carry good messages. But also keep in mind that what's good for someone else might not be good for you, or vice versa.

Write the good things here, and use this list to counter the negatives whenever they come up.

_____

_____

_____

_____

_____

_____

_____

_____

_____

_____

_____

_____

_____

_____

_____

_____

_____

_____

Notes

"I have learned silence from the talkative, toleration from the intolerant, and kindness from the unkind; yet, strange, I am ungrateful to those teachers."

—Khalil Gibran, writer

10. REPLACE TOXIC THINKING

Learned behavior is insidious if it's negative. If your mother was a yeller or used guilt to get you "under control," or your sister ruined your stuff when she was angry, or the older boy next door was basically a backyard bully, or your father lost his temper, or certain people in your family or neighborhood drank a lot, you might have learned that their behavior was acceptable (even if you did not enjoy it). Because you learned it in the past, you may not even realize that it is counterproductive, or that there is another way to behave or think.

▶ What we experience as children, or when we're vulnerable, can overwhelm us and create toxic thinking without our being aware of it. Using affirmations is a wonderful way to reprogram the toxic thinking toward healthy thinking.

In my own search to find ways to outfox my negative and toxic overthinking, I discovered that affirmations worked great. Doing affirmations is like adding water to fat or oil. The affirmations will sink deep within, the fat (toxic thoughts) will rise to the top and eventually can be removed. Keep in mind that the toxic thinking has been going on for a long time, and it will take a lot of repetitions of the affirmations to overcome it. This chapter will show you how.

Identify Your Toxic Thoughts

In the last chapter, you looked at the sources of your learned toxic thinking and overthinking. Now you'll create affirmations to overcome it. First, make a list of the negative thoughts that tend to trouble you. The list doesn't have to be complete; you can come back and add more later. Your negative thoughts might be things like "I won't do it right," "I'm no good at math," "I'm not smart enough," or "No one will love me." I struggled with always feeling that I didn't have enough time, so I wrote, "Time is running out."

Write down the negative thoughts here.

Develop a Corrective Thought

Now think of a correcting thought for each negative thought. What is the countering truth? My correcting thought about time was, "There is enough time to do what I need to do. I have plenty of time."

Write your correcting thoughts here.

_____

_____

_____

_____

_____

_____

_____

_____

_____

_____

_____

_____

_____

QUICK CALM

Studies show that singing releases endorphins, so tune in to some mellow music and sing your heart out.

_____

_____

_____

_____

Rewrite your positive thoughts from the previous page, tweaking them if you need to, and add your first name to each one. For example, "I, Tina, have plenty of time. There is enough time to do what I need to do." Or "I, (your name), do not have to be angry just because my father was. I can use the energy to do something positive instead." When you're done, you'll have a list of positive statements.

Use These Affirmations

What you have created is a series of affirmations. Choose one to start with and write it ten times. Each time you write it, a negative counterthought (your original toxic thoughts) will come up in response. Just write the affirmation again. (I wrote my most-needed affirmations on index cards and carried them with me so I could repeat them silently whenever I had a moment. I didn't know how many times it would take me to memorize my affirmation, so I ran with the thought "Forgive 70 times 7." Soon I didn't need to look at the cards, as the positive affirmations became part of my brain. Today, you could type them in your phone.)

1. _____

2. _____

3. _____

4. _____

5. _____

6. _____

7. _____

8. _____

9. _____

10. _____

Identify Ineffective Distractions

When troubled by toxic thinking and the other kinds of overthinking, people often distract themselves with loud music, podcasts, audiobooks, TV, social media, or endless conversations by phone with friends. While you're doing affirmations, however, it's important not to distract yourself with these and other sounds. You need to focus your whole brain on cleaning out the toxic thoughts.

Which distractions have you been using?

_____

_____

_____

_____

Your brain's reticular cortex serves as the gatekeeper for stimuli, either helping you pay attention to what matters or making you easily distracted. Writing is one way to help train your brain to focus.

_____

Set Times to Focus on Affirmations

Become intentional about doing your affirmations. Choose some regular times when you'll stop using distractions and focus on your affirmations. When you have a schedule, you're more likely to do the affirmations, and the changes will happen faster if you're consistent.

Write a schedule here.

_____

_____

_____

_____

_____

_____

_____

_____

_____

_____

_____

_____

_____

_____

_____

_____

_____

_____

_____

_____

One Affirmation at a Time

When you have done one affirmation enough that the toxic thoughts have stopped coming up, and the affirmation is embedded in your brain, move on to the next one, and write it ten times here. As you memorize each affirmation until it's a part of your mind and brain, move on to a new one. When you get through the whole list you made on page 150, you can create new ones. Each time you notice a new negative thought, counter it with a positive one. (There are extra pages at the end of this chapter for more affirmations.)

1.

2.

3.

4.

5.

6.

7.

8.

9.

10.

Practice Makes Rote

This may seem a little daunting at first, but as you practice, you'll soon find that your new affirmations are part of you, and whenever you're not focusing your mind on some task, they'll run like background music in your brain. I like to walk, and I've found that the affirmations take on the rhythm of my steps as I walk. I've also found that like magic, I was calmer, more relaxed, and less rushed. To my surprise, things seemed to get done faster, and I was no longer late in getting them done. People also "magically" began to respond differently to me.

What changes have you noticed since doing your affirmations?

_____

_____

_____

_____

_____

_____

_____

_____

_____

_____

_____

_____

_____

_____

Positive affirmations aren't the same as toxic positivity, where you talk yourself into denying, or putting a bright spin on, something that's been difficult. Instead, affirmations acknowledge your situation, and that you have what it takes to push through.

Congratulate Yourself on Developing a New Tool

Now that you've learned how to create and use affirmations, you have a tool you can use anytime throughout your life to counter toxic thinking and overthinking. Affirmations are like a deliberate, positive type of overthinking that will help you counter the negative type. I still have all my affirmation cards from many years ago. I kept them in case I would need them again, and I never have needed them, since affirmations now come automatically to me.

Celebrate this accomplishment by writing a congratulatory note to yourself here.

> **"Rumination tends to be eased if we learn to be mindful; if we are able to be aware of it, and understand how our own thoughts work."**
>
> —Peter Kinderman, psychology professor

Additional Affirmations

1.

2.

3.

4.

5.

6.

7.

8.

9.

10.

Notes

"People who come from dysfunctional families are not destined for a dysfunctional life."

—Bo Bennett, author

11. OVERTHINKING YOUR OVERTHINKING

Oddly enough, it's possible to turn your overthinking on itself and ruminate, perseverate, or worry about your overthinking, in which case it becomes a spiral, dragging you down and creating stress—but not doing anything to overcome the problem.

► This kind of overthinking is endemic in students who take Abnormal Psychology classes. When they are introduced to the concepts of mental illness, most of them start overthinking their normal mental processes, worrying if they're signs of mental illness; since mental illness is a distortion of normal mental processes, this is easy to do. (My Abnormal Psych professor used to say, exaggeratedly, "Mental illness is mental health writ large.") It's so prevalent in college that professors often warn their students about it.

You can easily do the same thing about overthinking: being fearful and worrying about it rather than using the information here to overcome it. This last section includes a recap of the steps used to overcome overthinking and will give you the final boost you need to be less fearful and more successful in stopping the problem.

Stop Worry and Anxiety

If you find yourself feeling anxious or worrying, remember: you learned to face your worries directly and turn the worry into a productive conversation with yourself. Ask yourself what you're worried about, then discuss workable solutions to whatever it is. It can be a current or new worry, or one you've used in earlier examples in this book. Once you have thought up a solution, act on it. Use your version of the four steps (express, evaluate, brainstorm, and check facts) from page 29.

Write an example here. Come back to this as often as you need to.

Stop Perseveration

You acquired the power to change your mind. You learned to identify the thought and resolve the scene that it came from by playing it over in your imagination, changing the thought, and then changing the circumstances. You then created a list of your steps on page 56.

Rewrite that list here. Refer to it as often as you need to and use this space to alter or revise that list, if necessary.

Stop Perfectionism

You learned to recognize when perfectionism gets in your way and what it has stopped you from achieving. You learned how to encourage and show kindness to yourself. You learned to have a beginner's mind and to lower your expectations. And you understood that you can correct anything you do that needs correcting, without self-punishment or drama.

Write about how you can do good work without putting perfectionist pressure on yourself.

Stop Obsessive Thinking

You learned to identify recurring intrusive thoughts and realized how they obstruct your thinking and daily activities. You learned to look for repetitive actions that go with the thoughts and to understand when you're obsessive. You learned to face the negative, scary thoughts and wrote kinder counterthoughts. You created affirmations and wrote them repeatedly to conquer the obsessive thoughts and take control of your thinking.

Write those affirmations here. As those become rote, add more as needed.

Stop Avoidance

You learned to identify your avoidance behaviors, to look behind them to find out what scary or unpleasant thing you're avoiding. You got ready to name and face your relationship demons, your activity demons, your expectation demons, and you faced them directly by writing to them, one at a time. You reframed the demons as misguided and learned to direct them to help you instead of block you. You also learned you can repeat this process until you have confronted every demon and turned it into a helper.

Write your list of conquered demons.
Keep adding to the list: you got this!

_____

_____

_____

_____

_____

_____

_____

_____

_____

_____

_____

_____

_____

_____

_____

_____

_____

_____

Stop People Pleasing

You learned to identify your people-pleasing behaviors, asking yourself a lot of questions to figure out what you think about those things. You wrote down anything you want to change and made some new choices that were more about what *you* want, which makes you more capable of communicating your wants to others. You reviewed your choices about your style, your home environment, and your daily events and activities to make them better fit who you are.

**Write what you learned about yourself here. This isn't a finite list.
As you grow and change and learn more about yourself,
it's okay to add to the list, modify things, or even cross them out.**

_____

_____

_____

_____

_____

_____

_____

_____

_____

_____

_____

_____

_____

_____

_____

_____

_____

_____

Stop Self-Sabotage

You learned to identify the negative feelings you had about yourself, where you copied them from, and who confirmed them for you. You learned to reframe the negative beliefs about yourself into positive ones. You wrote an introduction about yourself and read it over several times. You considered making changes based on this more positive self-view and how to counter negative things when people say them about you.

Write the most important things you learned about how stop negative thoughts and feelings here.

_____

_____

_____

_____

_____

_____

_____

_____

_____

_____

_____

_____

_____

_____

_____

_____

_____

Resolve the Origins of Overthinking

You investigated your past to figure out when you began to worry and overthink, and that often came from imitating an overthinker you were close to. You figured out what you picked up from the overthinker, and to talk directly to the overthinking and say how you're going to do it differently. You developed a habit of noticing when your thoughts are copying what the overthinker did or said. You also learned to replace learned problem thinking (toxic thoughts) with new counterthoughts, framed as comments to the original overthinker. You learned that toxic overthinking can come from culture, family, religion, school, and other early environments and lead to prejudice against yourself. You countered the prejudicial thoughts with more enlightened thoughts, and you also learned healthy and loving thoughts in these environments.

Write your positive conclusions about who and what you are here.

_____

_____

_____

_____

_____

_____

_____

_____

_____

_____

_____

_____

_____

_____

Replace Toxic Thinking

Using what you discovered in the previous chapters, you learned how to identify and overcome all the types of overthinking. You also learned about affirmations: what they are, how to create them, and how to make them a permanent part of your mind to push out toxic thinking. You wrote a list of your most troublesome thoughts, created an opposite positive thought, and then rewrote it in the form of an affirmation. You learned how to repeat affirmations to make them a permanent part of your mind and how to keep them with you so you could repeat them until they were fixed. You also learned how to stop masking the toxic thinking with various kinds of noise and how to change affirmations into a tool you can use any time you have bothersome thinking.

Write your affirmation process here.

_____

_____

_____

_____

_____

_____

_____

_____

_____

_____

_____

_____

_____

Take Control of Your Thinking

While you may not feel that you've completely stopped overthinking without more practice, you now know how. Remember, if any of these problematic thinking processes show up, you now know what to look for and how to overcome them. You can go back to the relevant chapter of this book at any time and review what you have learned. If you keep practicing what you've learned, you will soon be free of out-of-control thoughts and feelings. In my private practice, I always enjoy watching the stress lines slowly ease in my clients' faces and seeing their wonder at how people around them have "changed" in response to their new thinking. New, positive, productive thinking creates new, positive, productive lives. You are now free to build your own sense of who you are and create the life you want.

Write a thank-you letter to yourself, congratulating and thanking yourself for doing this work.

_____

_____

_____

_____

_____

_____

_____

_____

_____

_____

_____

_____

_____

_____

Congratulations!

You have freed your mind to be more productive and creative. You'll enjoy many fruits of this labor as your life progresses. In fact, take a few moments now and consider your life since you began this journey with these pages. Are you sleeping any better? Do you feel more at ease? Are you more creative or open to ideas and possibilities? Do you experience any symptoms such as headaches, heart palpitations, colds, or mood swings as frequently as you used to? The changes might not be as dramatic as that, but I can tell you they're there. You can pass on these skills to your children and, really, anyone else who wants to know why you're so calm and relaxed.

Use these last pages for any follow-up thoughts, questions, or issues you'd like to come back to, or anything else that comes to mind. Remember, these are tools you can use and reuse, any time you feel one or more of the types of overthinking creeping up on you. You can always counter it and give yourself peace of mind by using these tools. I'm wishing you happiness and peace, in a life that feels like your own, and a healthy partnership with your amazing, helpful mind.

Write down the changes you've noticed, lessons and tools you've learned, and summarize the journey you've been on to change how you use your own mind.

QUICK CALM

Laughter has been shown to release endorphins, those "feel-good chemicals" that help release tension and improve mood. For an instant calm, reach out to a funny friend.

Notes

Bibliography

"5 Acupoints for Anxiety You Can Administer Yourself." York Chiropractic & Oriental Medicine, 2023: yorkchiropractic.net/5-acupoints-for-anxiety-you-can-administer-yourself.

"Anxiety Disorders—Facts & Statistics." Anxiety & Depression Association of America, 2022: adaa.org/understanding-anxiety/facts-statistics.

Bratman, Gregory N., et al (June 2015). "Nature Experience Reduces Rumination and Subgenual Prefrontal Cortex Activation." *PNAS*, 112(28): 8567-8572.

Concordia University. "Surprising Truth about Obsessive-Compulsive Thinking." ScienceDaily, 8 April 2014: www.sciencedaily.com/releases/2014/04/140408122137.htm.

Cooks-Campbell, Allaya. "How to Stop Self-Sabotaging: 5 Steps to Change Your Behavior." BetterUp, 2022.

Curran, Thomas and Andrew P. Hill (2019). "Perfectionism Is Increasing Over Time: A Meta-Analysis of Birth Cohort Differences from 1989 to 2016." *Psychological Bulletin*, 145(4): 410-429.

Dixon, S. "Daily Time Spent on Social Networking by Internet Users Worldwide from 2012 to 2022." Statistica: August 22, 2022.

"How to Calm Down Fast." The Baton Rouge Clinic, 2021: batonrougeclinic.com/how-to-calm-down-fast.

Kushner, Robert F. and Seung W. Choi (Sept. 2012). "Prevalence of Unhealthy Lifestyle Patterns Among Overweight and Obese Adults." *Obesity*, 18(6): 1160-7.

Lally, Phillippa, et al. (Oct. 2010). "How Are Habits Formed: Modelling Habit Formation in the Real World." *European Journal of Social Psychology*, 40(6): 998-1009.

Lancaster University. "Social Media Stress Can Lead to Social Media Addiction." ScienceDaily, 27 August 2019: www.sciencedaily.com/releases/2019/08/190827125559.htm.

Lindberg, Sara and Kerry Weiss. "22 Ways to Calm Yourself Down." Healthline: July 20, 2022.

Nolen-Hoeksema, Susan and Zaje A. Harrell (2002). *Journal of Cognitive Psychotherapy*, 16(4): 391-403.

Pendry, Patricia and Jaymie L. Vandagriff (April-June 2019). "Animal Visitation Program Reduced Cortisol Levels of University Students: A Randomized Controlled Trial." *AERA Open*, 5(2): 1-12.

"Perfectionism in the Workplace." Momentum, 2022: momentumleaders.org/2022/04/14/perfectionism-in-the-workplace.

Rettner, Rachael. "The Dark Side of Perfectionism Revealed." LiveScience: July 11, 2010.

Rogers, Kristen. "The 4-7-8 Method That Can Help You Sleep." CNN Health: February 3, 2023.

Scholey, Andrew, et al (June 2009). "Chewing Gum Alleviates Negative Mood and Reduces Cortisol During Acute Laboratory Psychological Stress." *Physiology & Behavior*, 97(3): 304–12.

Schuler, Patricia A. (January 1999). "Voices of Perfectionism: Perfectionistic Gifted Adolescents in a Rural Middle School." The National Research Center on the Gifted and Talented: nrcgt.uconn.edu/wp-content/uploads/sites/953/2015/04/rm99140.pdf.

"Stress." The Cleveland Clinic, 2021: my.clevelandclinic.org/health/articles/11874-stress.

Suzuki, Sunryū. *Zen Mind, Beginner's Mind*. Weatherhill, 1970.

Waters, Flavie, et al (July 2018). "Severe Sleep Deprivation Causes Hallucinations and a Gradual Progression Toward Psychosis with Increasing Time Awake." *Frontiers in Psychiatry*, 9:303.

About the Author

Tina B. Tessina, Ph.D., L.M.F.T. (tinatessina.com) is a licensed psychotherapist in Southern California with more than 45 years' experience in counseling individuals and couples. Known as "Dr. Romance," she is the author of 17 books, including *52 Weeks to Better Mental Health*, and appears frequently in the media. She tweets @ tinatessina.

Quarto

© 2023 Quarto Publishing Group USA Inc.

This edition published in 2023 by Chartwell Books,
an imprint of The Quarto Group
142 West 36th Street, 4th Floor
New York, NY 10018 USA
T (212) 779-4972 F (212) 779-6058
www.Quarto.com

10 9 8 7 6 5 4 3 2 1

Chartwell titles are also available at discount for retail, wholesale, promotional, and bulk purchase. For details, contact the Special Sales Manager by email at specialsales@quarto.com or by mail at The Quarto Group, Attn: Special Sales Manager, 100 Cummings Center Suite 265D, Beverly, MA 01915, USA.

ISBN: 978-0-7858-4289-7

Publisher: Wendy Friedman
Senior Publishing Manager: Meredith Mennitt
Senior Design Manager: Michael Caputo
Editor: Jennifer Kushnier
Designer: Sue Boylan
Image credits: Shutterstock

Printed in China